THE UGLY
DUCKLING

A Story of Acceptance

Written by
Sharon D. Ulett, M.Ed.
Illustrations by **Mark Ruben Abacajan**

Order this book online at www.trafford.com
or email orders@trafford.com

Most Trafford titles are also available at major online book retailers.

Print information available on the last page.

ISBN: 978-1-4907-9009-1 (sc)
          978-1-4907-9008-4 (e)

Library of Congress Control Number: 2018953464

Our mission is to efficiently provide the world's finest, most comprehensive book publishing
service, enabling every author to experience success. To find out how to publish your book,
your way, and have it available worldwide, visit us online at www.trafford.com

Trafford rev. 09/06/2018

www.trafford.com
North America & international
toll-free: 1 888 232 4444 (USA & Canada)
fax: 812 355 4082

Acknowledgment

I would like to thank my family and friends for their continued support and encouragement.

I would also like to give a special thank-you to my doctor, Dr. David R. Smith, and my dentist, Dr. Michael J. Adams, two of my biggest fans, for always encouraging me to write the next book.

This acknowledgment would not be complete without thanking my mother, Vera A. Powell, for her prayers and encouragement and for reading my book, *Asheem: The Boy Who Could Not Read,* a hundred times or more.

I love you all.

One late afternoon, Celesta, a mother duck, went strolling through the high grasses toward the nearby Schuylkill River. She had sat on her four eggs all day and was now feeling a little weary.

"My, my, my," she said. "I really need a break. I am beginning to feel some serious cramps in my tush and legs. A swim in the river will surely soothe my aching body."

As she approached the river, a sudden movement startled her. With heart pounding, she hurriedly hid behind a small tree. Celesta could clearly hear the voices of two ducks as they argued.

"I don't think that's a good idea, Ann. Nothing is wrong with the egg," said a male voice.

"What do *you* know about eggs, Burt?" said a female voice. "Have you *ever* laid an egg?"

"You have completely lost your mind. You know what? I'm out of here, and I'm *never* coming back!" hollered the male voice.

Celesta could hear the male duck mumbling to himself as he passed by where she was hiding.

"Go ahead! I'll just do what I have to do!" yelled the female voice.

As Celesta stepped out from her hiding place, she could hear the female duck sobbing.

"What's the problem, dear?" inquired Celesta.

Startled by the voice, the female duck quickly turned around and asked, "Where did you come from? I thought I was all alone."

"I am so sorry I scared you, but I just wanted to know why you are crying. What was all the uproar about, and what's wrong with your egg?"

"You sure have a lot of questions for a stranger. Are you always this inquisitive? If you *must* know, my husband, Burt, has left for good because we had a disagreement about whether or not I should keep this discolored-looking egg," she said as she shoved the egg toward Celesta. "I don't think anything good will come of it. I told him I am going to roll it into the river, but he got extremely upset and left."

"Roll it into the river? Are you serious? I want you to take some time to think about what you are planning to do, young lady. Let's go for a quick swim. That will certainly help to clear your head."

"Go ahead, Ms.—"

"Call me Celesta," Celesta interrupted. "Now come along, Mrs. . . . What's your name?"

"My name is Ann."

"As I was saying, Ann, let's go for a quick swim. It will do you justice."
"Go ahead, Celesta. I'll be right behind you," Ann piped up.

As Celesta began to walk toward the river, she asked, "Ann, what happened to the rest of your eggs?" When there was no response, she turned around to see that Ann had disappeared. "No, she didn't! How could she leave her egg behind?" Celesta whispered to herself.

As she hurried over to where the egg was sitting on some dried grass, she shook her head in disbelief.

Celesta quickly pushed the abandoned egg with her bill all the way home and placed it in her nest with her four eggs.

Her neighbors soon gathered around the nest, gawking at the discolored egg. They sure had a lot to say. "Bad decision, Celesta. You are going be sorry!" Ms. Beatrice exclaimed. "How are you going to take care of five babies?"

"Mark my words, you have brought serious trouble on yourself, dear," said old Ms. Daphne.

"Listen, everyone. There is no way I could have abandoned the egg like that mother did. I just couldn't. Furthermore, this baby might turn out to be a blessing to all of us."

Celesta sat on her eggs for days. It was extremely hot during the days, so she would always go for an afternoon swim.

One day as she was sitting on her eggs, she heard a loud crack, then another and another. She hopped off to see that her babies were being born. All the eggs hatched, including the discolored-looking egg.

"Finally!" she said as she sighed with relief. "Welcome, my babies. It is sure nice to finally meet you all." Celesta proceeded to name her babies. The first duckling, she named Aidan; the second, Brian; the third, Leila; and the fourth, Lenamarie. As she got to the fifth duckling, she noticed something very strange. The little duckling, which came from the discolored egg, had a patch of black feathers on its back and head, and its little wings were drooping and dragging on the ground as it moved.

Celesta felt a strange sensation in the pit of her stomach. Ignoring it, she continued, "And you are Lucky, 'cause you are one lucky little duckling."

Celesta straightened their feathers with her bill, placed berets on the girls' heads and baseball caps on the boys' heads, then headed off with them in single file to introduce them to the neighbors.

"Meet my five babies, everyone!" Celesta yelled excitedly.

Ms. Beatrice and all the other ducks and ducklings stopped what they were doing and ran over to meet the newborn ducklings. "This is Aidan, Brian, Leila, Lenamarie, and Lucky!" Celesta continued, unable to contain her joy. "Aren't they beautiful?"

Suddenly, the place erupted in whispers. "What's wrong with him?" one voice said. "He looks soooo ugly, and what's up with the wings!" someone else exclaimed, followed by a giggle. "Hmmm! I did warn her about keeping that discolored egg, but she didn't listen," chimed in Ms. Beatrice.

"Enough! You've said enough!" yelled Celesta. "Now, I would like to start over. I would like you to meet *my* beautiful babies—Aidan, Brian, Leila, Lenamarie, and Lucky."

Everyone nodded in acknowledgment, but the looks of disgust were still visible. Some of the ducks walked away, mumbling to themselves. Celesta took her babies to the river, where they had a great time swimming and playing with each other. Lucky had a bit of a rough start, but he soon got the hang of it.

On their walk back home, the neighbors could be seen staring, but only a few made comments. The family passed a group of six ducklings by a tree. One of them yelled, "You sure are one *ugly* duckling!"

This made Lucky very sad, and as a lonely tear rolled down his face, he asked his mom, "Why are they being so mean to me, Mother? Do you think I'm ugly?"

"Oh noooo, Lucky! You are a beautiful duckling, and everyone will soon see that. We are all here for you honey. If anyone bothers you, they will have to answer to me," she said as she playfully rubbed her head against his neck.

As the ducklings grew bigger, so did Lucky's wings. This made him look even more awkward. It was evident to his family that he had a physical disability that could never be fixed, but they loved him anyway. All the ducklings, except his siblings, refused to play with him and continued to make unkind comments. The teasing was even more brutal at school.

One day, while at recess, someone shoved him into a large puddle of mud. As Lucky scrambled clumsily to his feet, a large clump of mud fell from his head and onto one of his eyes, covering it. His clothes were completely ruined. Lucky could hear them laughing uncontrollably as he walked home slowly, with his head hung low and tears streaming down his muddy face. No one came to his assistance. "Why does everybody hate me?" Lucky asked himself as he dragged his wings, which were even heavier with the mud. That night, he cried himself to sleep.

Another day while having his lunch all alone at a far end of the cafeteria, someone threw a leftover tater tot at the back of his head.

Lucky turned around to see who the culprit was, but everyone was busy eating as if nothing was out of the ordinary. As he got up from the table and headed for the cafeteria exit, more food was tossed at him. Someone also threw a box of chocolate milk, which got all over his new shirt. "Hey, how do you like your new tie-dye shirt, dude?"

Lucky turned to look in the direction of the voice. There stood the largest duckling he had *ever* seen.

"You sure look better now with food all over you, Ugly!" He snarled.

Lucky ignored his comment and continued walking out the door. He could still hear someone yelling, "And you better not snitch on me either!"

One day Lucky decided to go for a stroll. As he walked by some ducklings, the *big* duckling from the cafeteria ran over and snatched his baseball cap from his head. He took off running with his friends toward the river.

"Give it back!" Lucky yelled as he tried to catch up with them. His wings, which were extremely heavy, slowed him down a great deal.

"Come and get it, Ugly!" the duckling hollered over his shoulders as he burst out laughing. When Lucky finally got to the river, he saw a lot of ducklings swimming and playing. He splashed into the water and headed toward them. Lucky looked around the entire river for the duckling that took his cap, but he was nowhere to be found.

"Where did he go?" Lucky asked one of the other ducklings.

"He's over there!" shouted another duckling over all the commotion.

Lucky turned to see the duckling that took his cap smack-dab in the middle of a pile of twigs at the far end of the river. As he approached him, the duckling went under the water. When he resurfaced, Lucky noticed that he was tangled up in the twigs and that an old abandoned kite with strings was around his neck.

"Help! Help! Please help me, Lucky! This stuff is dragging me under." The duckling gasped as he went under one more time.

When he resurfaced, Lucky began to peck at the strings. They soon came loose. Lucky also used his bill to push the old kite over the mean duckling's head. Finally, the duckling was freed.

As they swam back toward the shore, the duckling said, "I'm so sorry for all the mean things I've done to you and for snatching your cap. Please accept my apologies. Here is your cap," he continued as he plopped it on Lucky's head.

Lucky removed the cap and gently placed it on the duckling's head. "You can have it, aah . . . what's your name?" Lucky asked shyly.

"My name is Dewey," the duckling responded nervously.

"Well, Dewey, my mom taught me to show love and respect to others and to learn to forgive. Therefore, I want you to know that I do accept your apology."

As Lucky and Dewey got to the shore, all the other ducklings ran over to them. "Why you hanging out with Ugly?" they all yelled in chorus. One duckling went on to say, "Aren't you scared that his ugliness will rub off on you?"

Dewey turned around, looked at them threateningly, and then said, "I want you all to listen to me. Lucky here is a great guy with a heart of gold. I almost drowned just now, and he could have let me after all we've done to him, but he didn't. Lucky saved my life!"

As a lonely tear of joy went slowly down his face and plopped onto Dewey's shoulders, Lucky smiled. He knew from that moment that he was going to be okay.

The other ducklings, one by one, went over to Lucky, gave him a big hug, and apologized for their bad behaviors. "I hope you can forgive us and accept us as your friends, Lucky," they said in unison.

"It's all good," Lucky said with a big grin on his face. "Now, let's all go and have some fun in the river."

Lucky, his family, and his new friends all lived happily ever after.

The End!

Printed in the United States
By Bookmasters